SIZE

by Brenda Walpole
Illustrations by Dennis Tinkler
Photographs by Chris Fairclough

LSCA student n/f grant

Contents

Gareth Stevens Publishing
MILWAUKEE

How big, how small?

Large and *small* and *heavy* and *light* are words we often use to talk about size. But how do we measure size?

The blue stamp in this photograph is larger than the pink stamp, so it covers more of the envelope surface. The blue stamp has a larger area than the pink stamp.

This doll is bigger . . .

than this one, which is bigger . . .

than this one, which is bigger . . .

than this one.

The largest doll has the most space inside it. It has the largest volume.

Who weighs more,
Laurel (on the left)
or Hardy?

When we talk about size,
we may be thinking of an
area, a volume of space,
or a weight, but it's not
always easy to tell how
big or small something is.
Could you say whether a
hippopotamus is bigger
or smaller than a giraffe?
What would you measure
to come to a decision?

3

Area

We can judge many areas approximately just by looking at them. Do you think there is enough pastry dough to cover the dish? But if you want to know how much carpet you need to cover a floor, then you must measure the floor accurately with a tape measure.

One way to measure an area is to divide it into small squares that are all the same size. This rectangle has been divided into twenty-four squares. Each square measures 1 centimeter by 1 centimeter. The rectangle has an area of twenty-four centimeter squares, which can be written 24 cm^2.

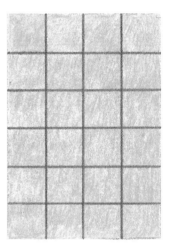

How would you write the area of a rectangle divided into eighteen squares, each 1 inch by 1 inch? With a ruler, draw some big and small rectangles on paper, using whole inches. Draw the outline of each inch square, then count them to find the area of each rectangle.

Make a chart like this to record the measurements of your rectangles.

length	width	number of squares (area)
20 in.	10 in.	200 sq. in.
10 in.	7 in.	70 sq. in.

Can you find a way of figuring out the area of a rectangle without counting all the inch (cm) squares?

Find the area of a leaf

You will need: graph paper, a felt-tip pen, some leaves.

Which leaf do you think has the biggest area? On the graph paper, draw around the shape of each leaf. First count the whole squares, then add up all the parts of the squares inside the outline. Did you estimate the area correctly?

Draw some triangles, rectangles, and ovals on the graph paper. Try finding the area of these figures using this method.

We usually measure small areas in square inches (cm^2) or square feet ($meters^2$) and use much larger measures for big areas of land. Land is usually measured in acres. The word *acre* comes from the Old English word for a field. One acre is 4,840 square yards (4,046 m^2), which was the amount of land that someone could plow in a morning. The aerial photograph on the right shows farmland divided into fields of a certain number of acres.

The metric unit of land measurement is the hectare. One hectare is equal to 10,000 square meters and is equivalent to 2.47 acres.

What's the area of this circle?

Find the area of a circle

You will need: a paper circle, a crayon, scissors, a ruler.

Fold the circle in half. Color one half, then fold it into four and then into eight sections. Cut out the eight sections and lay them out like this.

You have made a shape similar to what is known as a parallelogram. When you measured the areas of rectangles and squares, did you notice that the area equaled the length multiplied by the width? Find the area of the parallelogram using this method.

The more sections you make in a circle, the nearer the shape is to a rectangle. This circle has been divided into sixty-four sections. The length of the shape equals half the circumference of the circle. The width equals the radius of the circle. This means the area of a circle equals the radius multiplied by half the circumference.

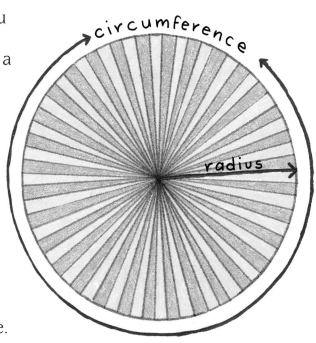

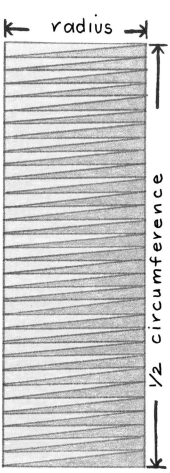

6

The pattern made by the pieces of material in the patchwork quilt below is called a tessellation. Each shape fits neatly into the next, with no gaps in between. The word *tessellation* comes from the Latin word for the small tiles used to make mosaic floors and walls, *tessellae*.

A tessellation is made by repeating the same shape over and over again. Tessellations can be made by joining simple regular shapes, such as triangles, rectangles, squares, and hexagons. Tessellated hexagons are found in honeycomb. Look for tessellated patterns in brickwork, mosaic, and tiles.

A tessellated pattern can be made more complicated by drawing designs on top of the basic shapes. How many different shapes can you find in the pattern above?

7

Volume

Some things are measured by their weight, but many are measured by their volume, which is the amount of space they take up. When people began to buy and sell grain and wine, they measured the volume of their goods in different-sized pots and jars. The volume of each container was the amount it could hold.

The ancient Greeks and Romans stored liquid in two-handled jars called amphorae, like the one in this photograph. The amphorae were different sizes, and some were used to measure amounts of wine or oil. The ancient Egyptians measured grain and wine in a container that held a cubic cubit of liquid. A cubit is the distance from the elbow to the outstretched middle fingertip.

The ancient Chinese measured grain and wine in containers that were carefully weighed and shaped. When the container was struck, it rang like a bell. In the ancient Chinese language, the word for grain measure, wine bowl, and bell is the same.

P.S. Find out what measures a bushel and a peck are. Can you convert these amounts into quarts and liters?

Today, we usually measure grain and flour in units of weight, but some goods are still measured by volume. For example, many recipes give amounts in tablespoonfuls and cupfuls.

Something to try

Figure out the volume of a cube

A cube has six square faces. In this cube, each face has sides that measure 1 centimeter.

A cuboid is a rectangular brick. If we arrange four similar cubes as shown at the right, they make a cuboid. If we put another layer of cubes on top, we have made a new cube. The space that the big cube takes up is called its volume. It takes up the space of eight small cubes, so we say it has a volume of 8 centimeters cubed, which can also be written 8 cm^3.

Try making some cardboard cubes with the sides of each face measuring 1 inch. Arrange four of these cubes to make a cuboid. Add another layer. What is the volume of the big cube you've made?

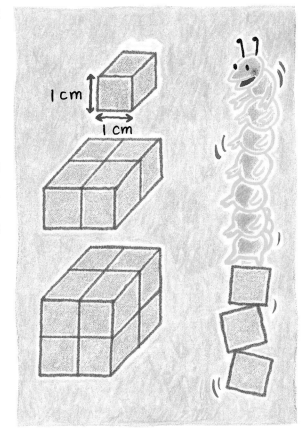

number of cubes along one side of each big cube	volume of big cube
2	8 cu. in.
3	27 cu. in.

A quick way to find the volume of a cube is to multiply the length by the width by the height.

Find the volume of a clay cube

You will need:
a glass measuring cup filled
with water, plenty of clay.

Make a big cube out of clay. Find
the volume of the cube using the
method described on page 9. Put
the cube in the cup and measure
how far the water rises. The volume
of the cube is the difference between
the first and second water level.
This process works because the clay
cube pushes aside its own volume
of water.

What happens if you squash the
cube into a different shape?

Find the volume of a small
stone using this method.

The story of Archimedes

In the third century B.C., in Syracuse, King Hiero asked the famous mathematician Archimedes to solve a problem. The king had given a goldsmith a block of gold to make a new crown, but when the crown was finished, the king was suspicious. Even though the crown was the same weight as the block of gold, the king thought the goldsmith had replaced some of the gold with silver, which was cheaper.

Archimedes thought that if the goldsmith had used some silver in the crown, the volume of the crown would be bigger than the original block of gold. This is because a piece of gold has a smaller volume than a piece of silver of the same weight. But how could Archimedes find the volume of the crown without melting it down into a cube again?

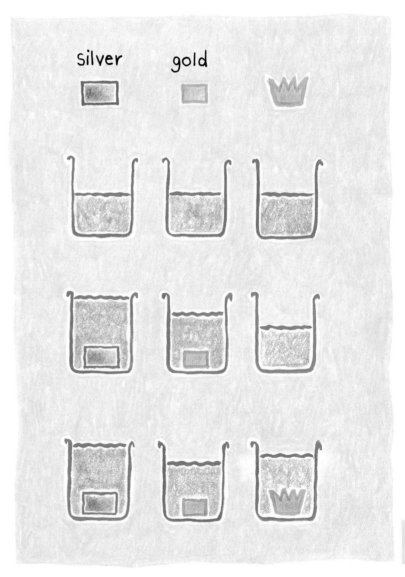

Archimedes filled three jars with the same amount of water.

In one jar, he put a block of gold that weighed the same as the crown. In another jar, he put a block of silver that weighed the same as the crown.

Then he put the crown in the third jar. The water level rose higher in this jar than in the jar with the block of pure gold. So Archimedes knew the crown was a mixture of gold and silver.

11

What's the capacity?

Liquids don't have any shape of their own, so they have to be measured in containers. The volume of a container is called its capacity. Today, many countries use the metric system to measure capacity in liters. A liter is the capacity of a cube measuring 10 centimeters by 10 centimeters by 10 centimeters. A liter is divided into 1,000 units called milliliters (ml).

The U.S. customary and British imperial systems use the units shown at right to measure capacity.

1 gallon = 4 quarts

1 quart = 2 pints

1 pint = 16 ounces

Under the imperial system in Britain, breweries in the past sold barrels of beer that contained thirty-six gallons. Smaller barrels were called firkins and held one quarter of the amount in a barrel.

In most of Europe, liquids are sold in liters only, but in the United Kingdom, some liquids are sold in pints. In the United States, people measure capacity in pints, quarts, and gallons, but an American gallon is smaller than an imperial gallon. The United States also sells some liquids, such as soda, in liters.

Collect different-shaped containers with a capacity of 2 cups. Check that you can pour the same amount of water from one to the other. Repeat with pints or gallons.

Something to try

See how much water a dishpan holds

You will need: a glass measuring cup, a dishpan, a shallow dish, a bowl, and a pitcher.

Estimate how much water each container holds. Pour in 1/2 cup of water at a time. Did you estimate correctly? Repeat using a measuring cup that shows cups and pints, adding one pint at a time.

P.S. How much water do you think you use every day?

13

Weight and mass

How much do you weigh?
When you weigh yourself on a
scale, a force called gravity is
pulling you down toward Earth.
All objects are affected by gravity.
When we say things are heavy or
light, it's because Earth attracts
them with more or less force.

In space, far from the pull of
Earth's gravity, astronauts
become weightless and can float
around. In this photograph, the
astronaut's feet are held firmly in
footrests to make sure he doesn't
float away.

On the Moon, gravity is only about one-sixth of that on Earth, so an astronaut weighs one-sixth of his or her Earth weight. Although the astronaut's weight changes, the "amount" of astronaut stays the same. This "amount" is known as mass. Every object has a mass, which is always the same, and a weight that can change according to the pull of gravity. On Earth, the weight of an object stays the same because it's always pulled down with the same force by Earth's gravity.

Although we usually measure weight and mass in pounds (kilograms) and ounces (grams), scientists measure weight in newtons, after Sir Isaac Newton. He was the first person to explain the effects of gravity. In everyday life, we give measurements of weight in pounds or kilograms rather than in newtons. This small mistake doesn't make our measurements wrong, just as long as we stay on Earth.

Weight in space

Each planet has its own gravity,
so a 110-pound (50-kg) person
would weigh:

— 442 newtons on Venus

— 500 newtons on Earth

— 190 newtons on Mars

— 1,330 newtons on Jupiter

How much does it weigh?

We have many sayings about the weight of things. Have you heard the expression "as light as a feather" or "as heavy as lead?" Light things are said to "float on air," while something heavy "sinks like a stone."

Estimate weight

You will need: identical plastic bags, marbles, rice, gravel, dried beans.

Take twenty marbles and put them in one of the bags. Fill another bag with dried beans until you think it weighs the same as the bag of marbles. When you have made your estimate, tie up the bags. Then estimate how much rice, and then how much gravel weigh the same as the marbles.

Check your estimates on a simple balance

You will need: a 1-yard or 1-meter length of dowel, string, a craft knife, bags of marbles and rice (see page 16).

Make a small notch in the center of the dowel and tie a loop of string around it. Hold up the dowel by the string to make sure the dowel balances. Make a notch 1 inch (2.5 cm) from each end and tie a loop of string around each notch. Tie the bag of marbles around one notch and the bag of dried beans around the other. Does the dowel balance? Was your estimate correct?

How heavy is air?

You will need: your simple balance, two balloons.

Blow up one balloon and leave the other flat. Tie a balloon to each end of the balance. What happens?

P.S. The air in an average-sized room is probably heavier than you.

Making it balance

The ancient Egyptians made accurate balances by resting a rod on a thin knife-edge that acted as a pivot. The object to be weighed was placed on one pan and the weights on another. This ancient papyrus from about 1250 B.C. shows a knife-edge balance.

Make a knife-edge balance

You will need: a long ruler, a triangular block, some identical buttons or coins, some clay.

Find the balancing point of the ruler and rest it on the edge of the triangular block. Carefully put a button on each end of the ruler. Is the ruler level? If the ruler wobbles too much, steady it with a small strip of clay.

What happens when you sit on a seesaw with an adult?

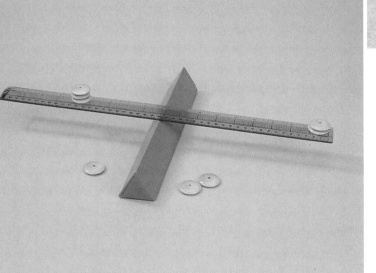

Try balancing big and small piles of buttons on either end of your knife-edge balance. Can you make it balance?

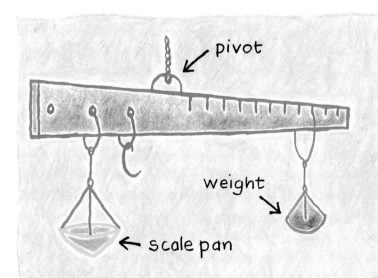

pivot

weight

← scale pan

The steelyard balance, invented about three thousand years ago, works much like the knife-edge balance. This illustration shows how a Roman steelyard balance worked. The balance was supported by a pivot that was not in the center. A small weight could be moved along the long arm until it balanced with the object on the short arm. The weight of the object was read from a scale on the long arm.

When you made a simple balance, you compared the weight of bags containing dried beans and rice against the standard weight of a bag of twenty marbles. The ancient Egyptians used standard weights, too. Some of these weights were made into the shapes of animals or people. This brass weight from Ghana is shaped like an animal.

In the nineteenth century in the United Kingdom, weights for kitchen scales were round or bottle-shaped. Each weight was twice as heavy as the weight below it in size. Make your own set of weights from marbles, clay, or wood. Make sure each weight is twice as heavy as the one below it in size, like the kitchen weights.

Spring balances

Babies are sometimes weighed on a spring balance like this one. The weight of the baby stretches a spring inside the balance. The more the baby weighs, the more the spring stretches.

Make your own spring balance

You will need: a corkboard, a tack, a spring, a paper clip or some thin wire, a strip of paper, clear tape, a pen, a set of equal weights made from clay.

Press the tack into the corkboard and attach one end of the spring over it. Stick a strip of paper beside the spring and mark where the bottom of the spring falls. Bend the paper clip or wire into an S shape and hook it over the bottom of the spring. Use your weights to make a scale. Attach one clay weight to the hook and mark where the bottom of the spring falls. Add another clay weight and mark the new position. Continue until you have a complete scale. What do you notice about the spacing of the lines? What happens to the spring when you take off the weights?

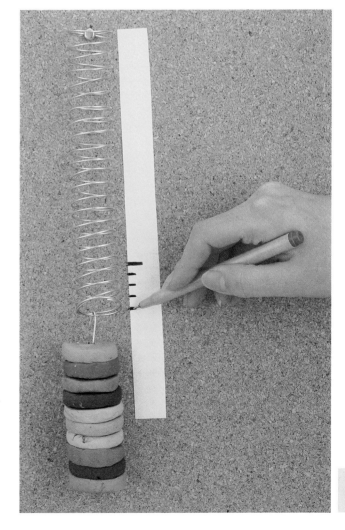

21

Squashy springs

The scale in this photograph also uses springs. When the fish are placed in the pan, a spring is squashed inside the balance. The distance the spring moves depends on the weight pushing down on it. Inside the scale, the end of the spring is connected by a gear wheel to a pointer that moves to show the weight of the fish.

Bathroom scales work in a similar way, but, because they may be used to weigh heavy people, they have stronger springs connected by levers to the pointer. The levers protect the spring and stop it from stretching too much.

In shops and markets, electronic scales are used to weigh food. When something is placed on the scale, an electronic signal is sent to a microchip, which calculates the weight and lights up the display. Electronic balances are also used in laboratories to make very accurate measurements.

Make your own top-pan spring balance

You will need: a large spring, two plastic containers that fit over one another, scissors, a strip of paper, a pen, a set of equal weights made from clay.

Make sure the spring is taller than the small pot. Secure the spring to the bottom of the small pot with clay. Stick a strip of paper onto the outside of the small pot. Place the big pot over the small pot and mark the point where the top pots overlap. Place one clay weight on top of the upper pot. Mark the new level. Continue until you have a complete scale. Use your top-pan balance to find out how heavy an apple and an orange are.

23

Pounds, grams, and grains

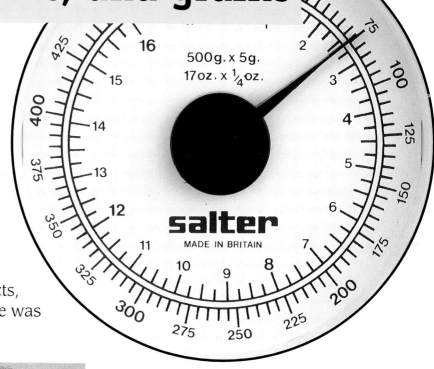

Today, most scales measure weight in either pounds (kilograms) or ounces (grams). In the U.S. customary system of measurement, the basic unit of weight is a pound. Originally, one pound equaled 7,120 plump grains of wheat. The pound was divided into sixteen smaller units called ounces. To weigh heavy objects, "stones" were used. One stone was equal to fourteen pounds.

In medieval times, sacks of raw wool exported from England had to weigh twenty-six stones.

The standard metric unit of weight is a gram. One thousand grams make one kilogram, which is a more useful measure for heavier objects. The standard gram has been set as the weight of 1 cubic centimeter of pure water.

Apothecaries were the first pharmacists. They used a special system of tiny weights to measure medicine. The smallest weight, called a grain, was the average weight of a seed of corn. Another weight called a scruple equaled twenty grains. This photograph shows pharmacists in the early 1920s weighing out the ingredients for some medicine. Now medicines are weighed in milligrams. A milligram is one-thousandth of a gram.

Centuries ago, Arab traders based their measures on a small bean called a carob. Today, jewelers describe the purity of gold in carats, which probably comes from the word *carob*.

Sometimes jewelers use a system of weights to measure gold, silver, and precious stones in troy weights. In this system, a troy pound is divided into twelve ounces. Originally, each ounce was equal to the weight of twenty sterling silver pennies.

Weigh the set of weights you made earlier on a scale. Do your weights increase in tens or fives — or a number that is more difficult to multiply? Could you use them easily to find the weight of an orange in ounces?

P.S. Use the chart at the right to convert your body weight from pounds to kilograms. Then try to convert your weight to stones.

1 stone = 6.35 kilograms
1 kilogram = 2.2 pounds
1 ounce = 28.3 grams
1 pound = 0.45 kilograms

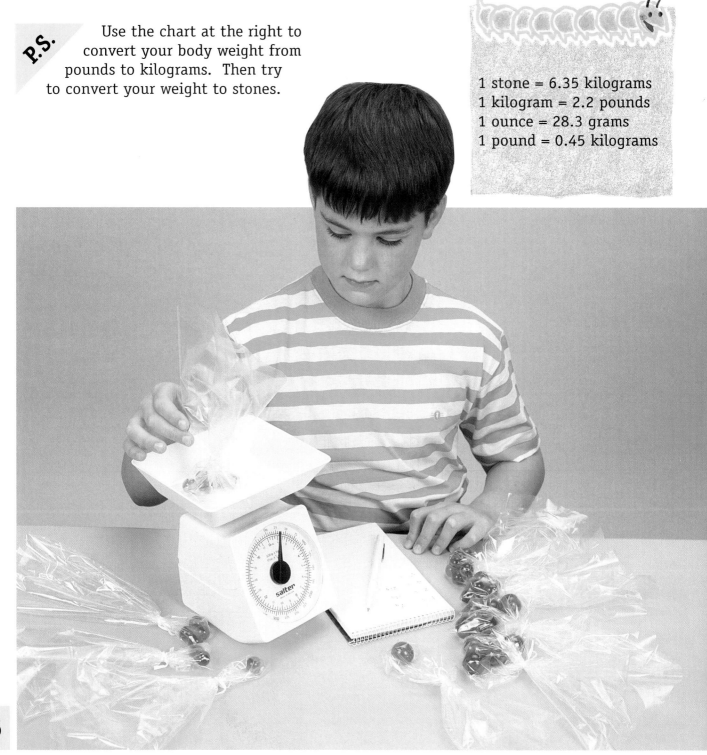

Changing size

Many things change volume when they are heated or cooled.
Most metals become bigger, or expand, when they are heated.
Some types of metal expand more than others. When the
metal cools, it becomes smaller again. This change in size is
small, but it can have powerful effects.

Metal bridges are always built with gaps between the
sections. Otherwise, in hot weather, when the girders
become slightly bigger, the bridge would twist and bend.

Liquids and gases also change in size when they are heated
or cooled. Inside a thermometer, there is a narrow glass
tube that contains either mercury or alcohol. When this
liquid becomes warm, it expands and is pushed up the tube.
The more the temperature rises, the farther the liquid travels
up the scale.

Water expands when it freezes. Ice takes up more space than water. In winter, if the water inside pipes freezes, it expands and the ice that forms is strong enough to burst pipes.

See how ice expands

You will need: a small plastic bottle, a piece of aluminum foil, water, a freezer.

Fill the bottle to the brim with water and loosely fit on a cap made from aluminum foil. Leave the bottle in a freezer overnight. What happens?

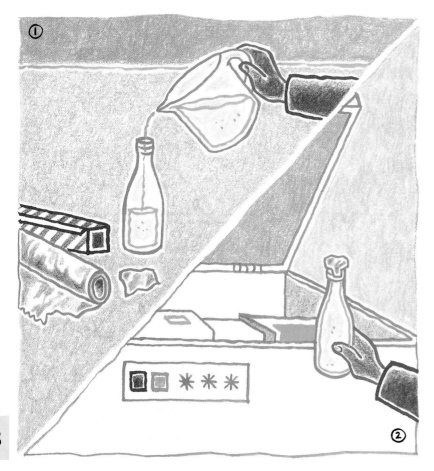

Growing up

Over time, most living things increase in size. Many plants, such as these sunflowers, grow taller and develop more leaves.

From the time we are born, we grow bigger and heavier, until we are adults. As we grow up, each part of our body grows in step with the rest. From day to day, you may not notice you are growing because it happens gradually, but you know you've grown when your clothes don't fit anymore or when you can reach a shelf that you couldn't reach before.

Important events

4000 B.C.

In Mesopotamia, the beam balance was being used. A beam was suspended from a central pivot by a rope. At each end of the beam, there was a rope. The object being weighed was tied to one rope and the weights to the other.

400 B.C.

The Etruscans probably invented the steelyard balance, which was supported by an off-center pivot. A small weight was moved along the long arm until it balanced with the object on the short arm.

300 B.C.

Around this time, Archimedes discovered how to find the volume of unusual-shaped objects.

200 B.C.

The Romans were using a unit of weight called the libra, giving us the abbreviation *lb*, which means pound.

1669

G. de Roberval from France invented scales that were later developed into the kind of scales widely used on shop counters.

1795

The metric system of weights and measures was adopted in France.

1824

In the United Kingdom, Parliament set the standard measure of a gallon as the volume of ten pounds of pure water.

1870s

Around this time, F. Sartorius from Germany patented a balance that was accurate to one part in a million.

1960

Electronic balances become widely available.

1964

The liter was defined as exactly one cubic decimeter.

1975

The U.S. Congress passed the Metric Conversion Act, calling for voluntary changeover to the metric system.

1975

Canada began a gradual changeover to the metric system.

1988

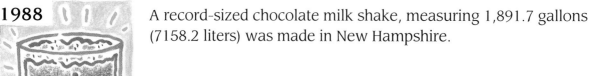

A record-sized chocolate milk shake, measuring 1,891.7 gallons (7158.2 liters) was made in New Hampshire.

1989

The largest hamburger on record, at 5,520 pounds (2,503.4 kg), was made in Seymour, Wisconsin.

For more information

More things to do

1. Archimedes discovered how to find the volume of King Hiero's crown as he climbed into his bath and water spilled over the edge. He leapt up shouting *Eureka!*," which is Greek for "I've got it!"

You can check the method Archimedes used to find the volume of gold in the crown. Take two identical cubes of clay. Use a measuring cup of water to check that the cubes have the same volume. Scoop out the center of one cube and fill it with plastic beads. Wedge the beads in place with some clay. Check that the sides of both cubes still measure the same. Weigh each cube. When you put the cube filled with plastic beads into the measuring cup, what happens to the water level?

2. Look at pictures of Islamic temples and architecture from ancient Egypt and ancient Rome. Can you find any tessellated patterns? Islamic patterns are often based on triangles and squares with other shapes drawn over them. Tessellated hexagons are often found in nature. Try to find enlarged photographs of wasps' nests, dragonflies' eyes, and the middle of sunflowers. Try designing your own tessellated pattern.

3. Find boxes of different shapes, such as toothpaste and gelatin boxes, that you think have approximately the same volume. How can you find out if the boxes are close in volume, even if they have very different shapes?

More books to read

The Biggest and Smallest. Anita Ganeri (Barron's)
Capacity. Henry Pluckrose (Franklin Watts)
Making Metric Measurements. Neil Ardley (Franklin Watts)
Weights and Measures. Robin Kerrod and Susan Baker (Marshall Cavendish)

Videotapes

Using Milliliters and Liters. (Coronet)
Measuring Is Important. (Barr Films)

Places to visit

Museum of Science and Industry
57th Street and Lake Shore Drive
Chicago, IL 60637

The Smithsonian Institution
1000 Jefferson Drive SW
Washington, D.C. 20560

National Museum of Science and Technology
1867 Saint Laurent Boulevard
Ottawa, Ontario K1G 5A3

Exploratorium
3601 Lyon Street
San Francisco, CA 94123

Royal British Columbia Museum
675 Belleville Street
Victoria, British Columbia V8V 1X4

Index

For a free color catalog describing Gareth Stevens' list of high-quality books, call 1-800-542-2595 (USA) or 1-800-461-9120 (Canada). Gareth Stevens' Fax: (414) 225-0377.

Library of Congress
Cataloging-in-Publication Data

Walpole, Brenda.
  Size/by Brenda Walpole; photographs by Chris Fairclough; illustrations by Dennis Tinkler.
    p. cm. — (Measure up with science)
  Includes bibliographical references and index.
  Summary: Discusses the elements of size, including height and weight, and explores various ways of measuring area, volume, and mass.
  ISBN 0-8368-1361-8
  1. Weights and measures—Juvenile literature.
2. Weights and measures—Study and teaching —Activity programs—Juvenile literature.
3. Size perception—Juvenile literature. 4. Size perception—Study and teaching—Activity programs—Juvenile literature.[1. Size. 2. Weights and measures.] I. Fairclough, Chris, ill. II. Tinkler, Dennis, ill. III.Title. IV. Series: Walpole, Brenda. Measure up with science.
QC90.6.W35   1995
530.8′1—dc20   95-21852

This edition first published in 1995 by
Gareth Stevens Publishing
1555 North RiverCenter Drive, Suite 201
Milwaukee, Wisconsin 53212, USA

This edition © 1995 by Gareth Stevens, Inc. Original edition published in 1992 by A & C Black (Publishers) Ltd., 35 Bedford Row, London WC1R 4JH. © 1992 A & C Black (Publishers) Ltd. Additional end matter © 1995 by Gareth Stevens, Inc.

Acknowledgements
Photographs by Chris Fairclough, except for: p. 3 The Ronald Grant Archive; p. 5 West Air Photography; p. 7 Gillian Clarke; pp. 8, 18 (t) Michael Holford; pp. 12, 19 (t), 21 (t), 22 (both), 27, 29 (t) CFCL; pp. 13 (t), 25 Beamish Open Air Museum; p. 14 (b) NASA; p. 20 Werner Forman Archive; p. 24 (b) Bridgeman Art Library; p. 29 (b) Mike Morton, CFCL.